COSMONAUT

A.E. De Vaul was born and raised in the Pacific Northwest, and later moved to first Cardiff and then Norwich. She currently lives in Wenzhou, China, where she is a lecturer in literature and writing.

She is an editor working with both *Lighthouse* literary journal in the UK and *Nimrod International Journal* in the USA. Her work has been nominated for the Pushcart Prize (fiction) and Forward Prize (Best Single Poem), and 'Broken Up', which appears in this pamphlet, won Eyewear Publishing's Fortnight Prize. Her first collection *Volcano* (2019) was published by Unsolicited Press under the heteronym Elosham Vog.

# Cosmonaut

A.E. De Vaul

*Valley Press*

First published in 2021 by Valley Press
Woodend, The Crescent, Scarborough, YO11 2PW
www.valleypressuk.com

ISBN 978-1-912436-67-5
Cat. no. VP0188

Copyright © A.E. De Vaul 2021

The right of A.E. De Vaul to be identified as the
author of this work has been asserted in accordance with
the Copyright, Designs and Patents Act 1988.

All rights reserved. No part of this publication may be
reproduced, stored in or introduced into a retrieval system,
or transmitted in any form, by any means (electronic,
mechanical, photocopying, recording or otherwise) without
prior written permission from the rights holders.

A CIP record for this book is available from the British Library.

Cover design by A.E. De Vaul and Peter Barnfather.
Cosmonaut photograph by Robert Couse-Baker.
Text design by Peter Barnfather.
Edited by Olivia Hodgson.

Printed and bound in Great Britain by
Imprint Digital, Upton Pyne, Exeter.

## Contents

Cosmonaut  9

Customs/Layover  10

Symptoms  11

Orientation  13

Trauma Theory  14

Foreigner  16

Respite  17

Language Lessons  19

Brexit  20

Intersections  21

Six pink pluses and so  22

Cosmonauts  23

Give and Take  24

Waiting for Plum Rain  25

Modals of Lost Opportunities
   with Two Missing Negatives  26

Deliverance  27

When flying  28

Ossuary: Bone House  29

dear valentina,  30

(   )  31

Broken Up  32


Acknowledgements  37

*To Valentina Vladimirovna Tereshkova,
the first woman and civilian in space,
who orbited the earth 48 times.*

# Cosmonaut

Dear Valentina: What do you think of
when you wake in the morning,
press your eye to the glass
and look out to see the earth spinning
in her orbit, inching farther then closer
then farther away? What to you dream
when you fall asleep in the glow of oceans
reflecting a sun you can't see?
Who do you talk to, when you hold
imaginary conversations; who do you see
in the television's black screen?
Do you ever want to step out
into the darkness, trust your tether,
let slip your feet, and float into the void?

# Customs/Layover

On the flight to Shanghai I learned
to say thank you, sorry, hello.
We touched down early and I sat
waiting until the aisles were empty,
grabbed my ukulele and stepped out
into the airport. I thought I'd see the city
but instead I saw the insides of my bags
spilled out over a conveyer belt, hands
sifting through, asking me about
the Star Wars bandaids and six books
of poems. Why did I need them?
I couldn't say; I watched the pages flipped,
took the books back with two hands
like a blessing at last: sorry, thank you, hello.

# Symptoms

There's something startling
about the spread of blood upon tissue,
the redness of it on hands or in sinks,
the residue left on tongue and teeth,
the salty iron tang.

He wants to know details
so I offer to show him pictures, the ones
I took for my doctor who speaks only Chinese,
and he laughs, says it's always freaky
to see blood where it doesn't belong,
which is anywhere other than cuts
or small scrapes. He's forgotten, again,
that I am a woman.
                        I want to tell him
about that other blood, the volume and
the surgeries and clots and pain and the babies
I didn't have and the babies I may never have.
But it's bad form, we don't show
our scars to colleagues on buses
or at restaurant tables, we don't discuss
such things on first or fifth dates. We lie,
I lie, about the purple and white puckers
each time I undress.

And if I can't tell him
about my aversion to doctors,
the tight spike in my chest
at that hospital smell, I can't explain
why I didn't go in for my next appointment,
why I'm willing to wait and see
if I get better or worse. And so I smile
to skate over the silence, shrug,
take a wheezing breath and pretend:
maybe next week, if I'm still coughing,
I'll go back for the TB test.

# Orientation

I climbed Yangfu yesterday,
ascended through layers of grey
dust and air to the viewing platform
at the top where I stopped
and coughed blood-streaked phlegm
onto the leaves of unknown trees.
I could see the river, the island
slanted at an angle to shore,
the factories and highrises and once-blue
roofs of builder's shacks, balconies
hung with shirts and cooking pans,
the cruise ship permanently moored
to the shore. And beyond them,
two shades dimmer, out of reach,
the dark streak of the sea.

# Trauma Theory

I.

It was the night we drank Oban
that wasn't Oban; Chinese baiju
in a hundred-pound bottle, served
with cheese from the import store.

Over cartoon cat mugs we talked
abjection, Lacan, the dark things
we humans inflict on each other,
toasted Kristeva with the dregs

of our disappointing bottle. I said
I loved it anyway, said I wanted
to fuck young Hannah Arendt
on her writing desk or on the street

if she'd have me: love, or something
like it. That's when he knew.

II.

That's not the whole story.

There was a guitar, a penny whistle,
a ukulele. Atwood, Morrison,
George R.R.'s underage sex. A bowl
of grapes, green globes swollen
and about to burst, the sweet scent
of our joints. His smile, that look
in his eyes, a possessive hunger
I wanted to fill – and the friend
who left when she sensed
that for us she was no longer there.

# Foreigner

When I walk through stores and board buses
a shush of voices follows, punctuated by the clicks
of mobile phones: lǎowài.

Lǎo means foreign but the wài is a mystery,
the character 老 alternately old, senior, a sign of respect
or a slight. An othering in any case, a signal

that I stand out. Sometimes I smile, sometimes
I keep my head held low, or pop up with jazz hands
into the shot. Sometimes I think of whispering

zhōngguórén, Chinese, back into the bustle,
wonder what I might hear in return.
But though I spend my nights writing

to you, I am no cosmonaut, no explorer
charting the unknown; I'm just a foreigner
who needs to learn more Chinese.

# Respite

That first week was delicious
torture, six long days and nights
of waiting for the blood to stop
flowing, the kisses to move south

In the mornings I pulled on polos
in the sticky heat to hide the dark
bruises spread like butterfly wings
across my collarbones

In the long afternoons we learned
to map moles and the pulse
of arteries across stomachs,
the places where sounds lay in wait

At night we curled close, didn't speak
of wives or endings or anything
other than desire and the love
we'd found in each other

Under patient hands and tongue
we stretched and unfurled
like flowers at the first touch
of sun, shared our dreams and smiled

a rarity for two people closed
tight as seedpods, transplanted
into parched soil in a city
brimming with watching strangers

We spent the seventh night panting,
limbs dead weight, heads heavy
on shoulders like shipwrecked sailors
who finally find a place to pause and rest

# Language Lessons

I.

*Breath* is the air that shapes
words, fills lungs; *to breathe*
is to pause and take it in.

II.

*Out of place* really means out
of *home*, means that *home* is
lacking or we are unwilling
to make it where we are.

III.

To be *queer* is to be open
to that which lies outside
some thing we call a *norm*.

IV.

To understand *branch out*, imagine
a tree limb or a stem, the splitting
of flesh to send out new sprigs.

V.

*Fidelity* refers to promises
we swear will never break.

VI.

*Back home* evokes what has been
left behind, the desire for a life
spent within the best of distant
memory.

# Brexit

My lover left me tied in bed
while he skyped his wife
on the shores of an England imploding

I could hear her laugh
coming from the living room
and I thought it tacky
that he didn't go
upstairs to his own flat
and leave me with my silence

You'd think it was a metaphor
or some sort of symbol

But it's just me, wrists worrying at knots
lying in the air conditioner's stream
wondering what he thinks
and when we'll begin again

# Intersections

In the mornings men dangle lines
into the canals, bare toes clenched
against cement buttresses
at the feet of bridges or splayed
across the raised pipes –
blue and black – that I imagine
carry fresh water and waste
from bank to muddy bank.
I can't ask, can't picture
the shapes they pursue.
What forms must swim
these undrinkable waters, what
secrets slip through the sheen
of salt pumped in from the sea?
And where do they go
once they've floated away?

## Six pink pluses and so

I imagine fish, the flutter
of fin and gill in a pacific
sea unpolluted by human
or animal; a patch of blue
water without oil or shit
or cesium-137, without
the churning trail of iron
warships chugging west
and east and circling shark
like in swelling schools
around what passes for
the wreckage of wings
in poems if not in bodies.

## Cosmonauts

Neil Armstrong said they saw
signs of others, heard voices
from across the vast seeming
dark before they turned white
clad backs to run; picture now
boot treads crunching into sand
in slo-mo, the scatter of sweat
and stone in rhythm with hearts
and the clenching of hands, eyes
fixed on the sealed shuttle door
and beyond it the long distance
to home; picture the confusion
felt and caused, the loss of all
certainty about their tiny world.

# Give and Take

My lover told me he
quite likes his wife;
he never said love.
He said he loves me, but

our love is a shadow
splayed across the walls
of Plato's cave, written
in verse with a shaking hand

on university letterhead
left pinned to my door
with a post-it note smile
as if it were a gift

as if I could return it
for a better fit.

# Waiting for Plum Rain

The mountains have emerged
from bifocaled smudges,
features – trees, dirt, outlines
of undiscovered buildings –
dotting grey sides.

In the courtyard a dog,
a fleshy bundle hanging distended
from his side like an organ,
pink, misplaced and shaking,
jogs across concrete.

In the classroom
ankles, knees, arms wet
with sweat, hoodies
lounged across the back row,
the slow rattling hum of a/c.

At lunch my colleague talks
about the new mall, the import
store in the basement, *real bread!*,
the clean-swept floors
and piped scent of perfume.

*We can make it to summer now*,
she says, and walks out into the sun.

# Modals of Lost Opportunities with Two Missing Negatives

    could     have
    should    have
         would have
    if I had    known

# Deliverance

Last night the sky split
with lightning, exposed
spine of the next highrise
tinged electric blue,
reflected in the pool of waves
where the courtyard will be.
I took the fruit from my table,
put it on shelves, replaced it
with bottles of water and a book
of poems, a towel nested in the arc
of the glass bowl. I cleared papers
and ukulele from the path
to the door, lit candles
and placed my umbrella,
one rib bent, fabric fraying,
on the wood before them.
I prayed for floods.

## When flying

I think of the radiation collected
stored in cells and hanging heavy
in thyroids so the singing throat hurts
Perhaps this is the story
the result of the sin
not of flying too high
or of seeking heaven but of hoping
to cross the borders of Babel
to speak to people born far away
and to be heard

## Ossuary: Bone House

Basilika St. Ursula, Köln: On seeing I am struck
by the thought that it's all about space, the gaps
between a shell of bone that once held hearts,
stomachs, lungs, lovers, the idea of holding

anything shown to be temporary or temporal –
an instant lost in a universe of vast time and
space, again, it always comes down to space,
to the emptiness that is not empty but a void

or vacuum, an absence that may still contain life
and that may yet be filled, whether it be with
atoms or cells multiplying or simply the shined
carapaces of beetles and a film of spiderweb,

not to mention the nails, metaphorical or cold
hard iron, holding it all together.

### dear valentina,

miscarriage
on the plane

what more
can i say

and so
the adventure ends

and i return
just the same

##                    (   )

( she would have
  had curly hair )

( she would have
  had his eyes, grey-green )

( she would have
  had a name from myth and legend )

( she would have
  danced like a poem from birth )

( she would have
  been my love )

# Broken Up

### I.

And so I stand
intestines spilling from my fingers
heart long scattered
to wind and the beaks of birds
who circle now, who see
the blood and the absence
spilling across the pavement

### II.

They've come home to roost
feathers sticking to ribs
and sternum, wingtips poking
liver and spleen
talons curled around collarbones
when they hang to sleep
like bats; some are bats
I can hear the rustle
in my chest, almost rhythmic
I can almost feel the warmth

III.

When I open my mouth
to sing mites pour out
trickle up my face to my hair
find homes, build nests
wave their legs in time
to the keen of jetplanes
and my battered ukulele


IV.

There's a sparrow
lodged in my throat
She shivers when I drink
sparkling water, screeches
at Oban and Laphroaig
but she likes the peat and sweet
of Lagavulin, coos and curls
herself into a ball so small
I could almost start eating again

V.

It's hard to ride a bike
when you've got birds
in your lungs
I cough up pinfeathers
and the hulls of seeds
on the bus, try to hide
my spattered hands
from the grandmothers
sitting silent around me


VI.

Pebbled eggs slip down
through my esophagus
tip and tilt from vertebrae
squeeze past my stomach
and through the ruins
to the cradle of my pelvis
I walk with hips held forward
to protect the fragile shells

VII.

In this city that lacks
the songs of birds
they're the last
of their kind, refugees
bearing witness
to a history
we'd rather wash clean
I can't help but cling
to their tiny bodies
can't help but feel
the urge to nurture
to never let them go

# Acknowledgements

Love and thanks go to Krystalli and Antigoni Glyniadakis for the gracious hospitality while I was working on this chapbook and other writing projects.

Several of these poems previously appeared in the journals *Amaryllis*, *Broad!*, *Mid-American Review*, *Prole*, *The Fenland Reed*, *The Interpreter's House*, *The Literateur*, *The Nassau Review*, and *Under the Radar*.

'Broken Up' won Eyewear Publishing's 8th Fortnight Prize, 'Language Lessons' was commended/shortlisted for the Bare Fiction Prize 2017, and 'Cosmonaut' was a finalist in Ooligan Press's 2016 Write to Publish competition.

The chapbook *Cosmonaut* was shortlisted in *The Comstock Review*'s 2017 Jessie Bryce Niles Chapbook Contest, and was a semi-finalist in Concrete Wolf Press's 2017 Concrete Wolf Chapbook Contest.